Praise for *The Swagger of Dorothy Gale & Other Filthy Ways to Strut*

"We dance with Sea Sharp in between the pages of this book and we are left spent and more realized by an ability to conjure such raw and unshakeable truths. We turn every which way, but loose, because Sea catches us up by expertly conducting gale forces. We turn each page to understand what it means to be the loneliest black girl in all of Kansas or what it is like to burn bright 'like the holy hallelujah of the sun.' We twist, because there's so much to witness when Dorothy is re-imagined and recreated as black, really black. She struts and we follow, because there's so much to learn about Sharp's Kansas. Sea imagistically swaggers and deftly leads us with wit. The choreography of wind, rain turned raging storm is brilliant in *The Swagger of Dorothy Gale and Other Filthy Ways to Strut*."
—Glenis Redmond, author, *What My Hand Say*

"A kind of postmodern country ballad, but realer and more fun, *The Swagger of Dorothy Gale* croons. Sea Sharp explores the many costumes and under-costumes that make up identity in the Midwest, writing, for example, 'I was a rodeo (I am a rodeo),' tracing not exactly the geography of our bodies but instead the geographies that our bodies can't help but be a part of. I mean, this book has it all: heart, imagination, and a good ear for the music we too often forget."
—Michael Mlekoday, author, *The Dead Eat Everything*

"'Dorothy Gale was really a black girl,'" writes Sea Sharp in this revisionist view of the *Wizard of Oz* family. This first book of poetry upends stereotypes of the American Midwest with swashbuckling language that delights as it informs and overcomes."
—Denise Low, Kansas Poet Laureate 2007-09 & author, *The Turtle's Beating Heart*

"Did you think you knew Kansas? Did you think it was Metro-Goldwyn-Myer, the Oregon Technicolor trail or bust? Nope. Black-and-white, degrees of gray, and the power of shoes and the dancing, strutting, bullshit-stomping, culture-journeying feet that can wear them or take them right off—Sea Sharp's buoyant poems kick at the margins and don't care if the roof comes down. By turns insouciant, clairvoyant, antsy and pissed-off, this collection sings, shouts, and shouts-out. Be sure to listen."
—Elizabeth Dodd, University Distinguished Professor,
Kansas State University

"Sea Sharp creates a surrealistic world in which the reader can ride the back of a twister and the sky becomes your momma. Imagination and the use of phonetically sound language become the sharpest weapon, as this collection attempts to survive and cope with the hardships of racism, stereotypes, and poverty. Sharp's poems give Dorothy from Kansas a necessary and relevant makeover!"
—Karla Cordero, Editor and Co-founder of *SpitJournal.com*

"Sea Sharp's opening epigraph, 'Cause magic won't work in Kansas,' spoken by Frank Baum's Dorothy Gale of *Wizard of Oz* fame, prepares the reader for a harrowing journey through a Kansas landscape—the Konza Prairie in flames, deadly twisters, sunflower fields, cottonwood trees—where 'Dorothy Gale was really a black girl,' and everyone is born 'with a bible belt wrapped around [their] necks.' Yet Sharp's book works its own magic on the reader, particularly in the penultimate poem, 'Slippers on the Shelf,' in which the opening lines, 'I, too have seen the gold of November sunsets' places Sharp in the tradition of Whitman, of Hughes, singing America. Sharp's *The Swagger of Dorothy Gale*, puts Kansas, long dismissed as a flyover state, on our literary and emotional maps.
—Donna L. Potts, Professor, Chair, Creative Writing Committee, Department of English, Washington State University

"Sea Sharp arrives just in time as an original, vibrant, and important voice. Their poetry in this debut collection *The Swagger of Dorothy Gales & Other Filthy Ways to Strut* gives voice—through re-imaging and deeply questioning the myths at the heart of one of America's most iconic stories—to history and politics, especially related to African-American women as well as prairie rhythms and dangers. All the time, they write with great music, a genius for dialogue and image, sharp critiques and bright wit, and in ways utterly powerful and tender."
—Caryn Mirriam-Goldberg, 2009-13 Poet Laureate of Kansas, author, *Chasing Weather: Tornadoes, Tempest, and Thunderous Skies in Word and Image*

"With uncontainable joy I ask the literary world to celebrate with me this striking debut collection of poetry from emerging author Sea Sharp. In *The Swagger of Dorothy Gale & Other Filthy Ways to Strut*, poet, naturalist, revisionist-self-exiled Midwesterner Sea Sharp harvests a bounty of language that allows the reader to sing with the cicadas, dance with sonic dexterity, rise with the corn, proclaim the vernacular as song and hymn. This collection will, quite frankly, 'Knock your breaths out.' Behold, a monument of new American poetry."
—Xavier Cavazos, author, *Diamond Grove Slave Tree* and *Barbarian at the Gate*

The Swagger of Dorothy Gale
&
Other Filthy Ways To Strut

Sea Sharp

*To Mariam
Thank you so much for wisdom. Much love.
— SEA.*

Ice Cube Press, LLC
North Liberty, Iowa, USA

The Swagger of Dorothy Gale & Other Filthy Ways to Strut
Copyright © 2017 Sea Sharp

ISBN 9781888160949

Library of Congress Control Number: 2016950683

Ice Cube Press, LLC (Est. 1993)
205 N. Front Street North Liberty, Iowa 52317 USA
www.icecubepress.com   steve@icecubepress.com
twitter: @icecubepress

No portion of this book may be reproduced in any way without permission, except for brief quotations for review, or educational work, in which case the publisher shall be provided two copies. The views expressed in *The Swagger of Dorothy Gale & Other Filthy Ways to Strut* are solely those of the author not the Ice Cube Press, LLC.

The paper used in this publication meets the minimum requirements of the American National Standard for Information Sciences—Permanence of Paper for Printed Library Materials, ANSI Z39.48-1992.

Made with recycled paper

Assisting Project Editor: Samantha Futhey
Cover Art: Marsha Craft

I would like to thank the editors of the following publications where these poems first appeared: *Crab Fat Magazine:* "An Autobiography in About 30 Lines or Less"; *Whirlwind:* "Black.Earth.Ling" & "Ground"; *Polychrome Ink:* "The Crackerjack Kid" & "Mombi Will Go to Prison Today"; *Sediments Literary-Arts Journal:* "The Prairie Witch"; *Three and Half Point 9:* "Obituary of Miles Davis"; *Storm Cellar:* "Journey of the Midwestern Queen" & "Tallgrass Shuffles"; *The Great American Literary Magazine:* "Trash and Bones"; *The Wild Ones:* "The Biography of Calamity Jane" & "The Llama Lady of the Barn Dance"; *Coe Review:* "Jonesy" (Previously titled: "Joansie"); *The Medical Literary Messenger:* "Burning a Hypothetical Helianthus Annuss"; *Blast Furnace:* "Sunflower Seeds"; *Flyover Country Review:* "Three Poems from 'The Swagger of Dorothy Gale'"; *NEAT.:* "The History of Booby Traps"

For Alex, the "best of swines."

THE CICADA ORCHESTRA

- 3   The Tallgrass Shuffles
- 5   The Llama Lady of the Barn Dance
- 7   The Biography of Calamity Jane
- 8   Midrusted
- 10   Trash & Bones
- 12   The Crackerjack Kid
- 14   Midrusted II
- 16   The Eye of the Buffalo
- 17   If Kansas is Your Bed
- 18   Mr Terrapene Takes a Shortcut Home
- 20   Manhattan Hill
- 21   Midrusted III
- 22   The Night is an Orchestra But the Glow
- 23   Burning a Hypothetical Helianthus Annuus
- 26   The Agoraphobic Describes Home
- 28   The Prairie Witch

AD ASTRA PER ASPERA

- 33   How to Swagger: An Introduction
- 35   An Autobiography in About 30 Lines or Less
- 37   Sunflower Seeds
- 40   The Swagger of Dorothy Gale
- 45   Retype From the Top
- 47   Legends of the Cottonwood Tree
- 50   Mr Terrapene Takes a Shortcut Home II
- 52   When Children Cut Their Own Hair
- 54   Poem for Billina's Menses
- 55   Almostly

57	Mombi Will Go to Prison Today
59	Behold! The Wonderful World of Color!
61	The City of Emeralds: A Bedtime Story

THE MIDWESTERN NEGRO JIG

64	Black Americana
66	Obituary of Miles Davis
67	Black Cats in Blue Rooms
68	The Robinson Sisters
69	Journey of Midwestern Queens
72	John Brown Returns For the #BlackLivesMatter Movement
75	Jonesy
77	Cig-Regrets
80	Poem for the Handbag Criminal
82	The History of Booby Traps
84	Black.Earth.Ling.
87	Ground
88	Slippers on the Shelf
94	Acknowledgements
95	About the author

Introduction by Debra Marquart, Prairie Seed Poetry Prize Judge

In the second section of Sea Sharp's remarkable new collection, the poet employs the Latin phrase, *Ad Astra Per Aspera*, which is also the Kansas state motto—*to the stars by hard ways*. This choice seems especially appropriate, given that the poems in *The Swagger of Dorothy Gale & Other Filthy Ways to Strut* take up the challenge of doing it the hard way, which is to say (in my mind) the Midwestern way, through iron and oxen and all night teeth-gritting kerosene-light staring at the unrelenting Kansas horizon.

While the poems negotiate this twin impulse of wanting to stay and fight for redefinition of place versus wanting to flee and save oneself, the poems articulate for the reader what it means to be ambivalent about one's home place. Maintaining this stance requires holding seemingly oppositional feelings in one's heart. The bold voice and the shout-out-loud vibrancy that breaks through in these remarkable poems rises out of that fraught space—at turns, claiming one's birthright, citizenship and fierce love for a place while also keening homeward from a position of expatriation.

This is why Dorothy Gale, the fictional character in Frank Baum's Oz novels and the protagonist in the film adaptation, *The Wizard of Oz*, provides the perfect backdrop upon which to project these poems of celebration, protest, and revision: "Dorothy Gale was really a black \ girl, if you want to know the truth. She woke \ each morning with Sunday shoes \ on her feet, and the grumpy Monday \ blues in her heart." Sharp continues, "And she was the most lonely black girl \ in all of Kansas, and

Kansas was \ the loneliest land of all." Like the narrator in these poems, Dorothy Gale was mutable and mercurial, forced to search and adapt to her changing circumstances. Dorothy starts out, an orphan growing up in Kansas with an Aunt Em and Uncle Henry who may or may not be her blood relatives. Nature forces her to flee, but she never forgets Kansas; she dreams of home.

Similarly, in the poems in *The Swagger of Dorothy Gale*, Sharp rewrites notions about what it means to grow up and make your home under this enormous mantle of open space: "last night the wind said \ be careful girl the \ moon be watching." Inside this maw of the prairie, "the sky can be your mama \ her rays and beams \ are lipstick smudges." But don't sleep too soundly, because "meanwhile hiding somewhere \ beneath your kansan cradle \ is the brittle skeleton of \ the konza and he is waking \ and he is stretching his jaws \ as the hallway lights \ snap off."

Both fear and awe lurk in that final image of the stretching jaw of the Konza, an expansive and ancient tallgrass prairie ecosystem, the remnants of which still exist in a protected 3487-hectare area in the Flint Hills of Kansas. But when Sharp speaks of the Konza it's to, I think, the primordial Konza, the geological cradle underlying what is now the Midwest, as it existed before the disturbance of Europeans and agriculture. On certain nights when it's quiet and the fading angles of sunlight are just right, it is still possible to feel the Konza, not so much as a sound, but as an inaudible tone, a vibration. Sharp's poems remind us of the magnitude of the natural world of the Midwest—so often undersung and underpraised—in whose overwhelming presence many of us live and work every day.

Similarly, when Sharp speaks of the tornado, a meteorological phenomenon forever associated with Kansas thanks to Frank

Baum, it's to both literal tornadoes, those cyclones that plague citizens throughout the middle corridor of America, but also about the metaphorical tornado, the whirlwind that roars like the voice of God speaking to Job: "Where were you when I laid the earth's foundation?" Sharp's voice rises off the page with that kind of love-licked ferocity. At turns, that voice sings, praises, struts, and scolds as it works to revise what it means to be a child of the Midwest.

In the amazing sequence of "Midrusted" poems, which take their lead from the Kentucky poet, George Ella Lyon's origin poem, "Where I'm From," Sea Sharp riffs, naming and defining a Midwestern origin story: "And I was corncob pipe. \ I was beef jerky and papa's \ chewing tobaccy. I was turpentine, \ I was matchstick. I was pocket lint." The enormous heart and voice and spirit that speaks in these poems is constructed of cobbled-together "rollingpins and bobbypins \ and auntie's blue muumuu," as well as the author's own spit, tears, blood, and bones. Indeed, many wonders are contained in this outrageously impressive first collection. Step inside and you will encounter "the whole damn state fair."

Debra Marquart teaches in the MFA Program in Creative Writing & Environment at Iowa State University and the Stonecoast Low-Residency MFA Program at University of Southern Maine. Marquart's work has received numerous awards and commendations, including the John Guyon Nonfiction Award, the Mid-American Review Nonfiction Award, The Headwater's Prize, the Shelby Foote Prize for the Essay from the Faulkner Society, a Pushcart Prize, and a 2008 NEA Creative Writing Prose Fellowship among others. Her books include *The Horizontal World: Growing Up Wild in the Middle of Nowhere* and *Small Buried Things: Poems*.

THE CICADA ORCHESTRA

"'Cause magic won't work in Kansas."

—Dorothy Gale,
From *The Road to Oz*
by L. Frank Baum (1909)

THE TALLGRASS SHUFFLES

last night the wind said
be careful girl the
moon be watching

said keep your fingers
out the mud keep your tongue
in your head said the moon

is watching you said she'll pull
you apart like the tide
when your time comes girl

rip out your womb like a second heart
drag it on the asphalt like roadkill
said you smell like roadkill

you taste like shit girl
said be careful the moon be
watching and she gone be mad

she gone tie you to the shed 'cause you
ain't primp enough for no ribbons girl
you ain't show girl you ain't top breed

you ain't pedigree girl
down girl bad girl sit girl
bangbang dead girl going

going sold just like that girl
the moon be watching so slow
down child said be still girl

said quit that noise
said stop that shine
said shuck that corn

girl she seen you bust the limestones brittle
do the tallgrass shuffles like dance moves
like prairie inferno hopscotch like shoooo

said ooooh girl stop playing
now smooth down your dress
and fold up your tail

and zip shut that grin
and pin back your ears
said the moon be watching you

said be careful said
swoosh and such said
heel girl said stay girl said die girl

THE LLAMA LADY OF THE BARN DANCE

i want to sweat with you
prairie wheat blooming
sway beneath moonbeams
no one can hear my prayers
and i'm promising you
woman searching for her
lads in the tight greased
seen you stepping tonight
big ladies with little voices
no like they are avoiding

and if i could cup your
girl but if my feet do not
to your back it is because
i need you to tell me my

if your legs smell like
brave witches waltzing
of the moon before they
of june but let us give it
yellow teacups small as
leave your beau and leave
take my arm and let me
into the pasture let me

tonight little twig of
between teeth as we
on the meadow where
may i have this dance
i will not stagger like a wasp
nest and i know the shameless
shirts will not step the way i have
and baby i cannot stand
always whispering nuh-uh-
someone's damnation

but not you–
you are a cabbage patch giggle

waist i'd roll you easy
move if my palms do not bloom
i am no gentleman
breasts smell like raindrops i
need to know
cinnamon sticks and we may never be
towards that electrical static-eyelash
hang us in the thick night jacket
a go let us tiptoe leave the scattered
thimbles gritty pools of cheap old wine
this barn
lead you
feed you

                      tiny kisses
                      barefoot stepping

and i really think   you could like it
with me

in little sips
pinkies pointing

                      to jupiter
                      and little sips
                      with me

THE BIOGRAPHY OF CALAMITY JANE

They used to call her a trigger happy bitch / grippin' one / no no / two ivory handled revolvers / gettin' buck-rowdy like Wild Bill lickin' / up the last drops of red liquor in saloons / and this gal / she got the sepia skin / she ain't beauty queen / she ain't Oakley girl with a western show like a damned act / grinnin' at Cody blowin' kisses like magic and tuhdah / no sir / not her / his gal / she got some dirt on her boots / got some grit in her teeth / and she patrols the whole frontier peelin' back scabs from her tiny bruised knuckles before she cracks them / pop / poppoppop / ohhh right on the nose / goddamn you motherfuckers / don't tussle with her fringes / don't rub trouble on her coonskin cap / she will clench her six shooters in her fists like oooh / yeahyeahyeah uhuh / and squishy explosions of heads splatter when she squeezes out that bangbangbang / it makes her grin like / shit her mama said / she used to be the sweetest thing / martha jane / pink cheeks blonde curls / yes sir the cutest shin kickin' / spit spatterin' / lil' lady of these here goddamn plains.

MIDRUSTED

I was a complimentary toothpick, a Saturday morning
yard sell, and a hand-me-down. I came from grandfather
clocks, and time with hands, limbs with needle holes,
lost teeth, black teeth, chipped teeth, and tear shaped
tattoos.

But I was born with mullet fever,
hair teased and a razor blade
on my tongue. I came from trailer
parks, from railroad tracks and truckers,
hitchhikers and hobos, bruises and scabs,
but I was the neighbor's sugar, an apple pie
on the windowsill. I was a sweetheart, a hayride,
a first kiss.

And I was corncob pipe.
I was beef jerky and papa's
chewing tobaccy. I was turpentine,
I was matchstick. I was pocket lint.
We are all sticky heat, a bonfire
near a scum covered lake, Bud Light,
Schlitz, Jack, cocaine, paint-thinner,
potato chips.

And I was the whole damn state fair.
I came from rollingpins and bobbypins
and auntie's blue muumuu. I came from

a pallet bed on a dirt floor, a hand stitched
quilt. I came from patches of fabric, knick knack,
paddy-whacked, gave a dog my bones, my spit,
my tears, my blood, my bones. I came from
rabbit skins and deer heads, up high, down
low, too slow. I came from sawdust and grit,
sweat and grit, raindrops and thimbles,
miles of barbed wire, and prairie and plains.
I came from the cattails of the ditches, the twigs
of the gutter.

TRASH & BONES

ONE. When she teeters into the bar,
this bone-jutted woman,
do not pocket your wedding ring.

TWO. Do not mistake her
for a burnt moth, sunken-cheeked
and thigh-gapped. Do not
let the barman sweep her
into the dustbin. It could take her hours
to wake up, wipe off her crumbs,
find someone sturdy, lonely, and mean.

When she smashes onto your table and oozes
onto your booth like a snowball slightly off target,
do not try to catch her. She will burst if you touch
her and she will make your skin sting.

THREE. When her pickup breaks down tonight,
do not reduce your speed. Do not take a look under
her hood. She will find the cut off sleeves,
the wife beaters, to lift her home. She will find brown,
callused paws on her tiny bent back,
scratching, grunting. Don't stop! Don't stop
for her.

FOUR. Don't let her
catch you
staring.

FIVE. Don't think about her
days off, with her kids who
wake up to nothing
in the fridge, who find
she's always out
of excuses, always
substituting the basics:

Water on corn flakes.
Butter in black coffee.
Cigarettes and time.

SIX. Even if she could drive
right out of this town, to "a big city
like Wichita," she will still beg for change like,
I wish I were, I wish I might…
Please. I need –please, sir, I need…

SEVEN. If she looks into your eyes,
do not adjust your collar,
and do not let yourself crumble into her lap
and weep. She will know
how to hold you and she will taste
of mother's milk.

EIGHT. Do not fool yourself.
If she were fixable she wouldn't be this knocked up,
beat up, "used to be daddy's little girl"
whose bones have always jutted.

THE CRACKERJACK KID

you could say i've talked about the weather
my whole damn life heard the train choo-chooin'
outside this town like a twister shufflin' through
like a drifter tipping pints who spills his hat and
smokes all over the goddamn floor like a whoops-
a-daisy so give 'em a hand boys and you can
call me frankie or billie or ponyboy or sodapop
or whatever the hell i'm warnin' you fella leave
my goddamn mother out of this goddamn you
we got four rusty oil drums out by the shed
and a fresh litter of kittens under the house
but mama shivers in the bathtub with her
catchpenny pearls she holds 'em in her palms
like tiny smooth confessions just prayin' for
somethin' good to come rippin' up her front porch

to wash her away and the folks always sayin'
put that big gulp down bubba boy and tell us
your goddamn story but i just keep on chewin'
my long red straw carryin' on like a juiced up mess
all wafer thin and shakin' all heathen
all crumble tongue all stink and they already know

how it goes and my pa was an outlaw who worked
in the salt mines he'd eat his lunchpail sandwiches
with a head torch and heehaw under main street
with his venous burble laughter goddamn it when

he'd reach across the supper table and pop
me one good for bein' a goddamn chucklehead
and oh how my brothers would snort their silly
heads off and oh dontcha know we lived
across the street from that old grain elevator
in hutch where the vertical storage was half a mile
long and as tall as the great wall of emerald city

but milkier than the holy holys that hold onto
everyone but just lets go of me and sister

she would shake her artichoke knees
all over the dirt yard back then and she
was the best goddamn prize in our whole
goddamn box

MIDRUSTED II

I came from six shooters and denim,
belt buckle and bandana, oiled saddle,
and ooooooooohhhh DAWGIE! You could say

I was a bank robbery, a horse, a buggy,
a wagon wheel, a freight train, depot.
I was a rodeo (I am a rodeo). I come from
(*move 'em on, head 'em up, ride 'em in,*
cut 'em out, call 'em out, ride 'em in) rawhide!

I was Johnny Kaw and Kaw Chief. I was buffalo
herd and outlaw, limestone, Osage Oranges,
and snake venom. I was a country western show,
a rope for a lasso, a rope for a lynching,
a rope to walk on, a line to cross.

And I was God and gospel,
a rickety pew, and amen. I am intelligent
design and Bible study. I am Heaven,
confederate heartache, Jim Crow -uh oh! I came
from barn dances and rag doll smiles,
eyeholes in sheet cloaks and "trick-or-treat,
smell my feet, bring me something good to eat,"
salt water taffy, molasses BBQ, Crackerjacks,
Bazooka Bubblegum, Cap'n Crunch.

I was an all you can eat buffet and a purse full of coupons.
I was barefeet on bicycle pedals, barefeet in gas stations,
barefeet on porch swings, dirty toenails climbing chain linked
fences. I came from a mouth full of soap and "Go and get me
some lemonade, child." I came from chicken coops and kittens
under the house, from mud pies and cow pies and cow tipping
and teepees in the woods. I came from tire swings and
playgrounds made of rust. From thunder that rolls like marbles,
laughs like hopscotch, skinned knees and skinned heads. I am
a pair of britches warshed in a crick, bursting with crawdads.
I was corn fed and grew some hair on my chest. I am a coyote.
I am a cicada orchestra.

THE EYE OF THE BUFFALO

it will derail you—knock your breaths out—
roll around the socket a little and topple out the skull—
bounce off the walls—down the halls—as the beast

                                        drops
                                        and then
                                        a rhythm
                                        sets in
                like chewing   around her bones
                or stabbing   and stabbing
                (and stabbing and stabbing)
or maybe   it's that violin vibrato—
or maybe   it's screaming for her life—
instead   of laughing
                at the punchlines—

IF KANSAS IS YOUR BED

then the sky can be your mama
her rays and beams
are lipstick smudges
marked on your face your temple

the chapel

but as that goddess called mama
leaves you tucked tightly
to the chin the door cracked
a smidgen safety light glowing

and nighttime wishes dragging at her heels

like a drunk purse
like a copperhead of the horrid oblivion
meanwhile hiding somewhere
beneath your kansan cradle

is the brittle skeleton of

the konza and he is waking
and he is stretching his jaws
as the hallway lights
snap off

MR TERRAPENE TAKES A SHORTCUT HOME

ground crawler
of the gravel roads
of the muddy horizon

belly scooter
thirsty one
searching for home

like an old man
squinting in a mirror
shocked at the brutality

of aging and how the wrinkling
crinkles everything poetry
and leaves all the beauty

to die there
like the dying
on parched tongues

and these days
he got
the pigeon's eyes

got the crusty
neck with many
miles left to go

and so many
more miles
to go

MANHATTAN HILL

Manhattan, Kansas:
A valley of named hills

from top this hill and top this enormous
letter-h / you can watch the redness soaking
into every tree / hear the leaves giggle-shaking
from their stems / hear the bustle spreading
through this undulating town / and even now

the whispers are swarming over everything / and even
now / they are screeching and scuttling / and off
they go / soughing around the valley like a plague
and the tuttle creek is a murmur-mumble
and to the vista drive-in is a burble-babble

and aggieville has just guffawed
and chuckle-snorted / and no one
can avoid this clumsy tinkle-knocking
of spoons swirling in a purple bowl of dust
all rusty colored foliage and last chances

and did you hear about linda /and did you
hear about bill / and the preacher said / oh
can you believe / the nerve of / good
lord / the rustle and the snicker
and the whistle scandal swishes

MIDRUSTED III

And I can still ride a twister's back,
grind a twister until my thighs turn black
and blue and I won't ever remove my grin.

I will always stomp the rubble when it's over.
And I was a pair of stretched and stained panties,
a pair of muddy boots in the bathtub gin.

And I came from garbage burned in rusted oil drums.
But nowadays I am just a thinned, floral print bed sheet
pinned up to a clothesline, flapping about in this strange space.

And when folks ask me where it is I come from? I will shrug
like a box turtle, fold a stray hair behind my ear and gaze out
towards where the hot pink sunsets should be.

THE NIGHT IS AN ORCHESTRA BUT THE GLOW

        the night is   an orchestra but the glow
bugs have just excused   themselves away wishing
to retire to chambers   urbane earthlings
gone off to mate   spoon their lover
move with rhythms   in the dirt shade
        like we do

the clicks and
the chirps and   on this unlit road
    nearby sleep
    nearby dawn

    oh see how   she loves
    to flutter   her wings like that
    and she melts   a little like
    a tart moth

BURNING A HYPOTHETICAL HELIANTHUS ANNUUS

I. one ounce:
>equivalent to 27 shelled seeds
>equivalent to 164 calories
>approximately one small handful

>>And if I run 22
>>minutes at 5mph,
>>my body can burn
>>like one small hand
>>-ful, like one ounce.

II. one head:
>an entire sunflower's head, depending on size, can produce 800-2000 shelled seeds, approximately 29.6296296 ounces- 74.0740740 ounces, and therefore contains 4,859 - 12,148 calories

>>It will take between
>>10 hours 43 minutes &
>>26 hours 47 minutes
>>of non stop running
>>for my body to burn
>>one head.

III. one speed:
>5mph = 12 minutes to complete a mile
>5mph = my "giddy up" speed

>>To burn the calories
>>of my hypothetical flower,

> I will need to run
> 53.58 - 133.92 miles
> as I giddy up
> into one speed.

IV. one race:
Dean Karnazes is a real person who ran
80 hours and 44 minutes without sleep,
(350 miles), equivalent to 3 days 8 hours 44 minutes.
Forrest Gump, who is not a real person, ran
3 years 2 months 14 days and 16 hours.
When Gump got tired he just went home.

> And I wonder
> how long does it take
> to spread myself
> thin?

V. one conclusion:
    To determine how many Americans, if placed on a calorie conscious diet, can burn one Kansan field of sunflowers entirely by consumption before the field's germination, typically within 5-7 days, an improved equation must be adapted. It is essential, therefore, to consider the following factors: human death rates caused by nut allergies, Basal Metabolic Rate (BMR), hypothetical food shortages, the average harvest, natural spoilage, bird and bug thievery, Standard American Diet (SAD) and other catastrophes. For example, if I ate nothing but one sunflower on a standard 2000 calorie per day diet, it would take me days to eat every seed although I have problems with leftover dinners and my nutritionist advised me to focus on portion control. I also

have poor balance and cannot run, therefore I will only consume one ounce of seeds, one small handful at a time and formulate new equations.

And I will watch in horror as I realise that every sacrificial face in this field is gazing towards the East, inspecting Mecca, seeking one conclusion as they all burn like the holy hallelujah of the sun.

THE AGORAPHOBIC DESCRIBES HOME

> *You haven't seen a tree until*
> *you've seen its shadow from the sky.*
> -Amelia Earhart

but the house i mean
trivial thing
stupidly built in a simple
place it is sensible and

it is small and it is woe
where did it go
it could disappear
like that i guess

if you sneezed on it
but chanute overshadows
the silly thing itty bity
bowl of dust

puts the runt to shame
and who would miss it
if it were hacked into bits
and never seen again

and would it make a difference
if the house i mean
were once a home i say
that is not the point

but the house i mean
and do not call it little
don't you ever call it little
i'll hit you on the nose if you call it little

but this house i mean this fragile
splintered hut was far more glorious
as the massive kansan prairie
and that i think is what i mean

THE PRAIRIE WITCH

not even the demented can shriek like the meadowlarks / who only rattle a little on my beak / strung necklace like everything / that is sacrifice / and we shall wear their feathers if we ever wish to fly / so pluck them all / clothe my boy in the colors / masquerade him as an inky sunshine bird / and i used to be an angel / you know

with the souls of the dead in my palms / like crystal goblets / i used to be an angel / but i never sip when i drink / i throw shit / i thrust my wings like *hell* / *i dare you to do a goddamn thing about it* / and everything's a sacrifice / you know

and you have to be careful down here / try not to eat all the woodrats / and when the copperheads and cottonmouths start rolling / down the valley do not move they will trip / us down beat us up / bruise our bones over those limestones / rip you into pieces / scatter you over on these hills like crusted drops of flint / you have to be careful down here / everything is sacrifice / and i used to be an angel / you know

but i should have been
a bobcat / chewing on the spines
of prairie dogs / lapping up the
streams / marking up the slopes / panting
in the shade of my den /
pleased and purring

but my wings look bomb blasted / in this place like amputations like flesh / and bone and skin and everything / is sacrifice and i work too damn hard / and i sweat so damn much these days / and i am putrid / and i am rancid / and i am cursed / you know

but tonight

icarus my little boy bird will learn to rise / and i will praise luna / singing *wallah wallayyyy weemama wallayyyy weemama* / and you can hear the coyotes weeping a lullaby / on the plains where i will disrobe / amongst my melancholy lovers / you will think my breasts / look nearly sacred beneath the orange of a harvest moon / and the blood on my hair will dry quickly / you know

and your anguish / cannot last forever / and the wailing / will just / you know

i was an angel once /
but tonight / i will sway
like a dying pregnant fawn / as the magnificent
konza bursts into flames like

hallelujah

AD ASTRA PER ASPERA
(To the stars through difficulties)

"Dorothy stood up and found she was in her stocking-feet. For the Silver Shoes had fallen off in her flight through the air, and were lost forever in the desert."

-From *The Wonderful World of Oz* by L. Frank Baum (1900)

HOW TO SWAGGER: AN INTRODUCTION

Dorothy Gale was really a black
girl, if you want to know the truth. She woke
each morning with Sunday shoes
on her feet, and the grumpy Monday
blues in her heart, and those funny
negro dreams in her head. And her

pigtails never moved, never flopped
when she walked and her hair couldn't
dangle, couldn't swing never danced
in the wind, but oh she could boogie
if you want to know the truth. She
could shake those boney hips and pop
that boney back and "UH-UH. No, child,"

Aunt Em say, snapping her fingers in
the girl's face, pulling a handful from
that kinky head through wide-teeth
and dragging it over a greased-up scalp
and yanks and yanks and yanks again
and then hot combs the whole room with that
smokey thick Louie Armstrong smile
all teenagers can dig. And Dorothy Gale

wore four braids back then if you really
want to know and they stuck out her
head shouting from end to end to end

to end. And she had no friends, no
friends, no friends to hold her hand
and skip on down the road. A lonely
girl with a stupid dog and a stupid family
on a stupid, stupid former plantation.
And she was the most lonely black girl
in all of Kansas, and Kansas was
the loneliest land of all.

AN AUTOBIOGRAPHY IN ABOUT 30 LINES OR LESS

they gutted my mama like a fish to find me
a sprouted pea-shoot reaching for the sun

i ran away when i was seven and nine clawed my way up
trees but they dragged me by the tail howling like a ghost

and i fell in love with a girl called annie i was five
and she had sunflower hands and a raspberry stain on her cheek

and i think maybe she loved me too but we lost touch
in the fourth grade and i killed my father slowly in my teens

he's still alive somewhere in oklahoma where the seagulls
won't find him and he's exactly where i told him to rot

and the doctors sewed my mama up as good as new
and she gets better like the wine she bathes in

and i've bled every month for about 30 years or less
putting off the melancholia this time but maybe not the next

and yesterday was my birthday and to my surprise
i discovered I was a corn snake in a black woman's body

and that explained so much at the time and ain't that a bitch
and sister was a chigger-bug if you know what i mean

all bite no hiss and nasty as hell and now
i'm married to a cowardly lion from oz

i left kansas just the way i found her
dusty faced and squinting and cupping both her ears

SUNFLOWER SEEDS

i bet we could fly away like thousands
of amelias / if we could just loosen these bonnets
and scatter our lovely ancient bones / over someone
else's grave before the wishes expire / and who could
blame us / and did you know that all the kansan queens

have been choked / we are all born with a bible
belt wrapped around our necks / and my god
she's calling the cross a "necklace" now / and oh
my lord / what were they thinking / letting their child leave
the house like that / have they no shame / these kids ain't
got no respect / but near our folk's little house
prayers are growing like weeds in the ditches /
wildly discarded like empty beer cans our marlboro
boyfriends would chuck out chevy pickup trucks /
as they'd drink and chuck / and drink and smoke
along those little dirty roads leading straight to nowhere /
in no place / and we still let the wind pull our hair out
the window / pilot our hand through the current /
bare toes propped on the dashboard / eyes closed /
humming to the radio static / but can you blame us /

and did you know that all the kansan queens
have cut their lips on the prairie / grasses
blowing their vertical harmonica whistles whilst they walk
barefooted / soles like leather treading and we /
have baked mud pie in the sun / and we have hunted

the crickets and the street cats and the lightning
bugs and never eaten a opossum / and we
are all the same / some are shy / some insane /
we take our secrets to the grave or to the chapel
or hang them / from telephone wires / let them
sing like wind chimes / sing like gospel / sing
like marvelous gray ghosts in the heartland /

so i never learned to do-si-do / but I could shuck
the shit out of any sunflower / rip it to bits / eat it
like a bird / spit the shells onto either coastline
if I wanted to / and I never wanted to breathe
like this / none of us choose to breathe like this /
sighing in reverse / preparing for the worst /
but can you blame us / this could have happened

to you / and every kansan queen has seen the sky
tinted green / and heard the thunder echoing
(it's echoing!) and we know the weariness
of neighbors poking onto porches / waiting
and waiting and / we have heard the sirens /
we know their warnings / but still race into
the middle of our streets wearing nothing
but cutoff shorts or ripped up shirts just to
watch the sky start spinning because
(it's spinning!) we all have drowned in the ocean
of the moonlight / coughing up our wishes / up
our childhood / up our days / and we still think
these bruises look pretty / and we still toss
hair clippings over the lawn / and we are still

stubborn / still eager / and feisty / and fragile /
and we are still the rustic colors of american beautiful /

and we are still here / on a front yard sofa / popping
off the ends of green beans for supper / and we
are so tired and there we go / dreaming ourselves
to death / but sometimes we still think of flying off
the coastline like amelia did / and can you blame us /
and did you know that / this could've happen to anyone /
and this could've even happened to you

THE SWAGGER OF DOROTHY GALE

I.
i did this
to myself

asked for it
pretended i

wanted to
come back

here

thought i deserved
deportation into

the Graylands

and desperation feels like fists
snagging grass petals it feels like life

has always depended on a single colour
that can never be my own and i predicted

all these ashes all this tooth rot predicted
the cancers the graphite the dead tarnished

eyes of park statues expecting all their pigeon's

shit kansas is Gray like this and

i predict kansas will always be Gray like this

II.
we know this Gray like the oldness creeping
over us like slow motion like forced smiles
on grandmothers remembering how they used to look

just the way you do child and no one wants to die here
it's true they tell you no one chooses to die
here but when the last drop

has been sipped and the last scone
has been jammed when it is time to return
your tiny serviette to the table where it was found

push back your seat and excuse yourself away
shuffle up the wooden stairs like your nana would do
put on your silver sunday shoes like your nana would do

and throw on a shawl and take your time and breathe
ease into your rocker like a hot bath sway as if
the wind from an open window were blowing you back

dig in those heels like you're being forced to go (go
back) back to that horrid Grayness you belong in
and it's true kansas is Gray tonight

III.
don't be fooled by all the shocked
faced shadows swinging from the branches
sad to say they ain't surprised
they knew their day would come like that
they planned their hauntings drew up
the blueprints with twigs in the mud
the night before their after parties
they hung up their streamers
mixed their punch
reviewed the guest list
chuckled into pieces

and you can find them in the city parks at night
queued at the little Gray water

fountains with *white* written with *black*
letters like it's all just an inside joke the living folks
seem to have forgotten nowadays but claim

to understand and i don't understand
why we are still stuck in this dust
bowl age sinking into grainy filmed pictures

we are pitchfork arms we are crosses burning like
hallelujah we smell like tar we vomit feathers
and i don't think it makes anyone *color blind* to see

it is so damn Gray here they call this *black and white*
but it's just Gray here can't you see us starving

like the africans we let the flies bite our bones

like we are africans we dig in the dirt or sweat
on our porches praying because all this sunshine
has been filtered straight from heaven sad to say

it's true that the holiness
is smudged away and god's thumbs
are ever so distinctly tinted Gray too

RETYPE FROM THE TOP

outside the cars are asleep in their ditches and the opossums
have dug into the bins and are fighting with the cats and it's autumn 1993
and it begins with you

and me sitting in the kitchen
looking across
this poem

as if it is writing this act
and all the scenes in it

one beat
then you sigh push
back your seat leave the table cross
upstage right shuffle out turn out
the lights

cue the dimming
lights on me

you have gone
backstage
to bed again
this time the props master strokes your hair and says
you are the only person I've ever met who really understands me
I never thought I could feel this way I've never told anyone this but cut

that was a typo that
is supposed to be my line

another cold reading to run-through more editing
to erase and erase and blow away
our miserable ending
to the drawing board we rewrite
retype from the top and action

LEGENDS OF THE COTTONWOOD TREE

> *"There are Cottonwoods*
> *on the Great Plains today that were*
> *living when the great herds*
> *of bison still roamed the prairie."*
> *-Jim Mason, Naturalist*

I.
Terrible clones sent for war,
sinister spawn of the prairie beast,
Mother Tree, the Cottonwood,
seasonal breeder of angry seedlings
that chase children across playgrounds,
an airborne zombie-ism, like terrorism,
like "I am going to KILL you!" and
make the world snow covered,
a Christmasy April, a magical cruelty.

II.
Youths in mid-skip,
in tether ball tugging bliss,
unprepared at recess by how
the enemy travels with the dust,
how downy soldiers, incognito
in the wind, clobber noses, smother
the back of throats and classmates
are choking on the soccer field, some
are on the ground dying, spread out
on a foursquare patch, chalk lined; this

is not a homicide, this is a massacre
designed to destroy us one class grade at a time.

III.
On weekends, Oma read us stories
from the Fatherland: *"Der Wind, der Wind,
das himmlische Kind!"* Tooth-gapped and grinning,
we'd spin and spin, stumbled and bumbled, silly
and dizzy like it was one of us, like it could be one of us!

It was witchcraft, the way we summoned the air
to stroke back the cotton, budding from the branches.
And we spent entire hours sprinting across the backyard,
praying for "Oly-Oly Oxen" and "Jesus Christ" to spare us all
with no tag backs because you have to play fair and no!
And stop! And redo!

IV.
The stupid ones, left behind,
in their nose crusted, pee
stained glory, climb to the top
like she is a jungle gym. They try
to "tame" her, but are too ignorant
to start choking, too dim to even
sneeze. They breathe easily, whilst
wailing under her branches, which
demand them to "shove off!"

At suppertime these children murmur
to their mothers about scraped elbows.
They play with their peas and potatoes,

And plan tomorrow's attack.

V.
Blame it on the hay if you wanna, mama,
but when we sneeze like Cottonwood
victims, eyes puffed and itchy, noses
dripping and snotty, the kids on this block
will know where to point their grubby fingers
and these kids already know summertime is due.

MR TERRAPENE TAKES A SHORTCUT HOME II

when aunt em say
he ain't comin' in her
house "unless he's stayin' for supper"

dorothy reckons she's found herself
a new friend / pulling him to her chest with
anxious grubby hands / he just curls deeper
into / his black and yellow coat / red eyes rolling
around / like an ancient god in meditation / emptying
his bladder onto dorothy's new school clothes /

aunt em cackles
her blackened teeth
squealing
like the violins of a hitchcock murder /
scene / licking her lips she balances
herself off the front porch rocker /
toto on her heels / set to boil / a pot
of water and lets the screen door
slam back / those simple needs and
immodest desires / desires /

desires / but somewhere in kansas
a small girl / with a sinking / dampened heart
in her chest / suspects she'll see her friend again /

and uncle henry
won't even know the difference

WHEN CHILDREN CUT THEIR OWN HAIR

Countless tragedies will probably happen:
1) Parents will divorce each other.
2) Non-masculine people will be called bitches.
3) Some bitches will get raped.
4) The smartphones of non-rapists
will shatter or malfunction
or just stop working
for no apparent reason.
5) Some mythical king
from a non-fictitious land
will marry his own mother
on accident and mutilate his
own eyelids on purpose.
6) Birds will poo on people.
7) People will poo on themselves,
but diagnose it as bird flu.
8) The hicks who kick down the rainbows
will scrape the bloody glitter off their boots
and win.
9) And ZZ Top will finally break up.
10) Airplanes might collide into buildings.
11) All the rum will be gone.
12) And some drunken, imbecile in the corner
of auntie's darkened parlour room
will knock over a rim-filled cold
and delicious glass of beer
and it

will fall
in slow
motion
while the Midwest
like the hair of unattended children
playing with scissors
will just continue
to disappear

POEM FOR BILLINA'S MENSES

to think
i'll grow

you in
a cavity

hollowed out
tumor-being

every fudge
brownie crumb

wasabi pea
spoonfuls of crunchy

peanut butter
the perfect binge

potential life is
this junk

this junk is
done desire

but you are new
a recycled nothing

ALMOSTLY

Dorothy got the duct taped shoes.
Got the trash bag slicker. Got patchworked
real good and keeping dry. Keeping fly. Almost.

And Uncle Henry ain't nobody's daddy,
but he puffs his Camels and learns to read
the newspapers at night, but mostly almost
by candlelight. And Toto won't shut the hell up; damn
dog, bowwows at the curtains, shuttering.

And Auntie Em ain't nobody's mama, but she can
waterproof a Dorothy Gale every springtime
like a mama. And she got Dorothy raking leaves,
got Dorothy pulling weeds, got Dorothy beating rugs
like a mama. And Auntie got them mama hips. Almost.

And Auntie rests her fists on her mama hips when
the lips pucker-pout, when the tears drippy-drop, when
Auntie ain't gonna tell ya again, child. When she done
had it up to here, and she fed up now, so go'n. When
she say she gonna tell ya Uncle if ya don't get and
straighten ya self up real damn quick... Auntie don't play.

Auntie wears a mama glare now. And Auntie shoots lazers
from her mama eyes, blows dragon smoke from her mama
nostrils and Auntie can hex a Dorothy with her wicked
pointer fingers. And Auntie's face say she fix'n to snap

ya chicken-neck, if ya don't quit act'n a fool. Her face say I'll pop you, but her heart say I love, I love, I love, Dorothy, Dorothy, Dorothy, almost, almost, almost...

MOMBI WILL GO TO PRISON TODAY

but her mother has baked sweet potatoes
for the Bible study, vacuumed the sofa, and replaced every baby
photo with pictures of white elephants. She has painted her lips
fire engine plastic, outlined them like a crime scene, dressed up
for a funeral, or a prayer, or an apology.

When the Sisters arrive too early, bringing pretzels
with cola, Mombi's mother will hold her tongue
between her teeth, hold her breaths in her chest like heavy
secrets. She will sit on a metal fold out, thumbing
the golden ridges of her New World
Translation, confusing scripture
with Watchtower, remembering her baby witch or "local
monster." She will search for redemption,
find torn newsprints, rub the ink into her fingerprints.

When the conducting Elder turns to Second Timothy,
the congregation will gasp and the sound will crack like locusts
slamming into the windows. They will let their eyes roll around
to visions, to proof and prophesy and prayers for Mombi's
three lovely victims.

"Let us shake hands, eat chips, look joyous,"
the Brothers will say and plan car groups for afternoon
Field Service. They will dodge puddles in the hallway,
wipe their mouths on their sleeves, grin at the lightning.

The Sisters will speak in circles. Their skirt hems will gravitate away
from their ankles as they spin like wind chimes before a storm.
And the children, bold horseflies, they will tango
on tiptoe, skip and squeal, and paddycake romp.
They will speak in tongues and set fire to the puzzle rug.

And Mombi's mother is a grubby
faced rag doll thrown behind the sofa.
Her lips are a paper cut factory,
her silence, another guilty verdict.

BEHOLD! THE WONDERFUL WORLD OF COLOR!

The perception of color is one of our most pleasurable experiences. YOU are about to enjoy the most sensational and most technologically advanced colors available in the world today. NOW! With even more intensity!

It seems pretty silly to have taste buds but no flavors. Why have sight but limited, boring colors? Colors can help neutralize dullness and help improve physical appearances when in contact with light. For free color downloads visit, www.wonderfulworldofcolor.com and experience our collection of vintage colors like "mauve," "foam green," and "magenta"! Or upgrade your account to Premium and be the first to see "bleenuff," the very first Certified Synthetic Glow (CSG).

No artificial ingredients. No preservatives. No chemical solvents or yeast. 100% kosher. Not tested on animals. Suitable for vegans.

Suggested Use: Allow one splash of color into eyeball until accustomed to its sensation. Repeat this procedure with other eye. Repeat both steps *again* until you are able to perceive multiple colors simultaneously. If irritation occurs, close eyelids until relaxation returns and try again. Please do not exceed three primary hues a day.

WARNING! CAUTION! Do not use if shades are broken or missing. Please consult your physician before exposing yourself to extreme hues such as the electric or neon varieties! If you are pregnant or nursing, highly intoxicated, nearly dead or no longer living, a canine, or undergoing extreme psychotherapy, you may be unable to enjoy "The Wonderful World of Color."

If you have difficulty seeing color as effectively as others, this may be caused by a hereditary color blindness. Do not adjust controls in your eye socket. If the muted effect of blurry gray or blindness occurs, simply apply water to dilute, then rinse. If color is not retrieved to original intensity, YOU WILL NOT RECEIVE A REFUND, NOR WILL YOU BE COMPENSATED. Please keep all colors out of reach of children. Do not consume colors unless they have been securely attached to food or beverage. This product may cause a severe allergic reaction, especially in people who are allergic to light or color. Symptoms may include: facial swelling, racism, hallucinations, watery eyes, blindness, vitiligo, flamboyant homosexuality, magic, or death.

Do not apply to leather, suede, velvet, corduroy, vinyl, plastic, or silk unless valid license is obtained.

Questions or comments? Call toll free: 1-800-IC-COLOR

MADE IN USA

THE CITY OF EMERALDS: A BEDTIME STORY

From the painting of Theodoor van Thulden, "The Allegory of the City of Antwerp," c.1640s

Legend tells us that *she* was the first zombie ever created—therefore the first dead thing to ever kill. She tempted the first fresh thing she saw, bit everything that moved. And back then every god knew a monster and back then every monster had a weakness and back then it was all ebb and flow, and to and fro, and ying and yang, and harmony (so to speak), but no god fought a zombie back then. No zombie ever died back then. And so the city commissioners held their meeting at the end of the month. At last, they decided to throw *her* into the snake pit because a city planner had a good idea and said, "Hey, guys! I know what we should do. We can just dump her in that snake pit over there." And it was unanimous. And they all agreed. And the snakes ate her insides. And everyone thought, "At last!" and "Thank the gods—the zombie queen is dead!" and "Whew! What a relief!" and "That will be the end of her," but it wasn't. Any living creature can become a zombie (just think of the dinosaurs). And so the zombied snakes wormed themselves into her brain. And her skull was like the shell of a thousand headed turtle. And they worked together. And they spoke to her, at last.

She was the first zombie ever known, the first dead one to keep living. After losing the heat in her toes, losing the balance in her legs, she learned how to slither in the dirt, in shame. In the meantime, she could always hear the whispers in her head that said she was a monster. The voices said, "Just look at yourself.

You are a monster." And behold, at last, she was. And despite all the chatter, she felt so alone. And so she asked the boy with the magical darts to help her, but he would not. And so she asked the man with winged shoes to help her, but he would not. And so she slinked to the feet of the mayor, rolled onto her back, and begged, and begged, but the voices with words that itched her ears for understanding, they said, "You are a monster. The city needs you to be their monster." And she understood it all (at last). If no one is wrong, then no one can be right. And if no one ever lied, then the truth would be useless. And if the night isn't dark, then the day is never bright. And if the hate doesn't hurt, then the love doesn't soothe. And so she became the most terrible thing imaginable because it was the right thing to do. She did it for the city. She did it for herself. And as she was assaulting Chronos near the walls of the city's cathedral, the tongue of her tongue sliding around in his ear, the voices, they stopped whispering,

and all of them moaned in terrible ecstasy, at last.

THE MIDWESTERN NEGRO JIG

"So if you pay no attention to these peoples, you may never hear of them again."

—Glinda to Princess Ozma
From *Glinda of Oz*
By L. Frank Baum (1920)

BLACK AMERICANA

You probably think my melanin is a driveby, is a food stamp,
think my melanin is drug bust, is gang bang, is murder,
"but my melanin is golden baby," my grandmama say,

"My melanin is super-
stition, is superpower.
So my melanin is power."

Word? 'Cause my power is a fistpump
to the Lord. It's a thank you. It's respect
and a Hallelujah! Amen! It's a cannon

from the north and it's a lemonade in the sun.
It's a railroad beneath the ground that doesn't make a sound.
And it's meeting dead ends and making ends meet.

And my melanin can shmoney, can dougie, can jerk.
My melanin can tootsie roll, stanky leg and twerk.
And you know I keep it fresh, and I'm the freshest, and I'm dope.

And my melanin keeps the ripe, strange fruits
from bursting when that beat drops. And my melanin smells
like tar; tastes like cornbread and collard greens.

And I've got so much of it. And I've got more than you.
And I've got enough to go around. And I've got enough
to turn a white man's child several shades of black and brown.

I've got melanin for the masses, melanin for the pope,
melanin for the white kids shooting
up the schools. This melanin is a gift.

It's American Beautiful. And it's not just a color. It is ancient.
It is mother. It is healer. It is manna. It is burdon.
And it's my melanin, (yeah, this, all of it)—this my melanin.

OBITUARY OF MILES DAVIS

just a "boy"
approximately thirty-one years
a Negro five shades darker than
Afrika, 6'1" maybe more
(probably less)
trumpet playing
son of a bitch

self-loathing ego-
maniac fist pumping
faces of lucky females
pinned punched stuffed
until the legend's brew falls blasé
and dumping his bitches
into the hallway for the maids
to toss out is the only way
to "finally get some fucking
work done"

just the "blues"
sixty-five years
an Afrikan Ameri-can't
stop a brotha this black
5'9" maybe less
(not more)
trumpet playing
son of a bitch

BLACK CATS IN BLUE ROOMS

For Dr. Wayne E. Goins

the spotlight casts her shadow on his face
she's sing'n the blues 'cause he's warm'n up
the mouthpiece with smoooooth lips that blow with taste

gesticulations that revive the dump
an improvisational ensemble
lost in the feline howl of the trumpet

and in that special way fingers humble
to all 88 that help "play that shit"
thebass willthump abeating thatquickens

and they'll dance then rest for a second round
no one can explode until it thickens
and then the clap'n and whistle'n will sound

they say all great things might break but can mend
and a black cat will play until the end

THE ROBINSON SISTERS

These old girls throw their heads
back in slow nods to the rhythm
of their rocking chairs. To
and fro. To
and fro. "You show
is grow'n like a weed,"
one croaks to the street
ball boys, playing too rough. "Look'n
just like they mama," the other agrees. Then
their blue-haired heads bob
and raise on the front porch
of their slanted home.
They sip on sour lemonades in the thick,
Kansan heat, while flicking wicker fans
in their gnarled, ancient grips.
They'd flick their fans,
and bounce blue heads,
and rock those chairs sluggish.
Each of them mum'lin' and hummin'
something sweetly to Jesus,
"Lawdy, Jesus!" To
and fro. To
and fro.

JOURNEY OF MIDWESTERN QUEENS

I.
It is forbidden to offer this kind of science in classrooms.
To speak of the rainbow like this, is to encourage
madness, but don't be fooled by their arches.
They are fully circular in shape, chronic banded, ringed,
half exposed in the sky, half hiding underground,
like ostrich heads in sand, like so many people
in a sultry wardrobe.

II.
When the Queen is forced to leave the homestead,
she will ask for time to pack her cases, to brush the horses.
She will paint her nails, pinch her mother's
favorite pearls and leave
her muddy boots in the bathtub.

She will remember to kneel before the altar
of her nanna, reciting a final litany.

III.
Tonight at six, Pastor Simmons will pray
for the damnation of our souls, live on Channel 4 television.
He will tell all 200 people in his congregation and 300 viewers at home
to bow their heads, and clasp their hands, and beg for the Lightning
of the Terrible to strike down boys like us. And this is why we go
extinct in these towns, afraid of all the rain and the rumble.

IV.
After the Great Flood, God gave Noah
an apology: a flag with a stripe
for every tribe of love.
He called the first band "Agape".

V.
When the Queen reaches the city, her people
will be waiting like it is a prophecy, like she
is their Queer Messiah. She will call them
The Family. They will straighten
her hair, bedazzle her heels. There will be a parade
then a festival. Some will camp out, pitch tents, vogue.
Some will feel the fever in the streets, bend over the trunks
of abandoned cars, while many more will revel in their own
normalcy. They will hold their children close and promise
to love them always and always, Amen.

VI.
When she wakes up on Sunday mornings,
a smeared and glittered mess spread over
her man's lovely chest, the Queen will think:
Maybe it is possible
to live happily after all.

VII.
Sometimes it takes years to realize
that God never left the farm. He is still sitting there,
next to the remote control on that coffee table back home.
Like so many other loved books, there

to pass the time, he will wait eternity for you
to just "come on up to the house."

JOHN BROWN RETURNS FOR THE #BLACKLIVESMATTER MOVEMENT

> *"I, John Brown, am now quite certain that the crimes of this guilty land can never be purged away, but with blood."*
>
> -John Brown, 2 December 1859:
> The day of his execution

I.
When I realized John Brown was executed
the same day as that freed negro woman back in Kansas
who was forced to have "relations" with each Brown son
John fathered, I muttered under my breath, "fuck 'em."

And I knew I wanted all seven of his sons
dragged out behind a dumpster, wanted them
shaved and bleached, tongues snipped off,
screaming. And I knew I was turning
against my instinct to please my first
so called abolitionist who offered to be
another white saviour and if given the needle,
I question if I could strap down any
Supremacist and inject him like another
euthanized patient upon the table.

"If you don't fight us," they snarl
at black womxn, at Latinx, at me,
"it will be over soon." But if we pocket

these promises like milk teeth,
our grandbabies will still be fed
an injustice, a compromise,
a death.

II.
The night Trayvon was shot
I was in line at the drive-thru praying,
"for another tragedy, for a different terror."

I told the menu board, "yes," at the time
I thought I wanted to taste every GMO
under the sun and glow green like this

was an initiation, was a coercion,
was the police telling you to point
at the goddamn black guy

and so you point
at the goddamn
black guy

like this could be Mayberry
or Maycomb or someplace confederate,
and taking responsibility can mean taking

your own life, and taking the wrong turn
can mean crashing the Black Panther house party.

And I wondered whose ass would old Pottawatomie Brown
bust a cap in tonight? A white cop? A white collar?
The whole delicate system: White privilege?
Although everything crumbles beneath
the power of colors,

the fulcrum of this matter
is not blackness, it's dignity,
but to get the job done,

we need something bigger
like a Jesus and a Midol,
or a Snickers and a trigger.

JONESY

show me how to steal
black panties from the Walmart / stash
the grass and run faster when they chase us
up / the chain linked fences

show me how to be callused soles
kicking / a cow treading / the gravel
roads show me how to lose / time kiss
black boys in the moonlight / stick a quarter
in the payphone to feed our parents
lies and make them sound / delicious
because we must act first
play hard / live by the code

and I will keep
my shirt on

let us hold hands / you and I
walk all over this damn town
so everyone will see us
wild / enough to not give our fucks
away

show me how to walk
the long way home / like the street
kids in the ditches / grinding
their teeth / rough eyed and

starving / hitchhiking to
anywhere but here

and show me how to mock
the stoop kids / melting tenderly
three steps above the sidewalk
bible in their palms / feeling so much
closer to their dandy / white gods

CIG-REGRETS

PART ONE:
Balance it
in a scissor-
fingered grip
like the movie stars
flirting with small talk
and sips of burnt coffee
and always look cooler than
you feel and always feel pretty
damn cool mindlessly tapping ashes
off the tips man don't ever give a shit
and in the winters that gnaw on fingerbones
and in your gorgeously frost bitten hand it is
sometimes impossible to separate the "fresh air"
from all the casual poisons.

PART TWO:
Do you remember when professor would tip us
into his marigold dish? Burning like sacrificial offerings
on his bathtub shoulder? And each member of the
committee liked to give us a good thump over
their desks. And we'd laugh and bounce around
the lips of delirious doctors, putting a wicked grin
on their devilish camel's face. And I was only forty
cents a pack back then, muskier too. Wrapped in
cowboy leather, or bourbon, or gin, or sex, entertaining
the dinner party while the records would spin and spin and boy

could I boogie back then! And do you remember professor
had a Shag Wag? He'd drive us around to the point, follow me
to the back seat, unzip his pants, take a long drag, shake his
head about and call me his little stone fox, you dig?

PART THREE:
One day they will ban you from the water coolers
and deem you a diseased lot needing quarantine.
They will take you to court and the magistrate will
tie you to a post outside and tell you not to whine.
The entire office will call you a bitch. The judge will
tell you to bark like a bitch, pat you on the bottom,
give you a bone and no one will say this is
"separate, but equal" and no one will say this is
"smoker's rights" so gather your four minute
families close, and pigeon dance together along
the alleyway turf. Be mindful of the wind and
the eyes of your kin. And if Linda needs a light,
get to digging quickly. There are plenty of Bics
to flick amongst this Kali cadaver and plenty
of cupped hands to shelter any dying spark.
In a few years
you will sink
into the mud
when it rains
& finally learn
your place.

PART FOUR:
we are sinners

huffing like lunatics
dogs licking their
vomit a condition
another nauseating drone

we are Patron
Saints of Mumbling
Church of Ventriloquism
telepathy tinker's blood

this is not
a new language
i speak of
this is what
holy sounds like
as it burns

POEM FOR THE HANDBAG CRIMINAL

"It's suspicious leaving handbags on buses" they'll say
and the crone in sandpaper sandals will extend her bony
finger, pointing you out in the lineup,
scrunching her face like a cringing raisin.

In the enormous room, they'll shine hot lights
into your pupils, make you identify the bag
like a body, an autopsied carcass: mobile phone, tangled
pair of earbuds, 34 hairpins, yellow Bic, red Bic, book
of crinkled poetry, and forty tons of sand.
They'll ask
if you smoke.
You'll lie.

They'll say "if you don't
cooperate, you'll never see
your handbag again." A bluff.
They've got nothing. Stay cool.

They'll say "poetry is flammable."
"Yes," you'll agree.

Bad answer.

They'll throw your bag across the
universe as your entire life
flies before your eyes and shatters.

You'll call this "a hate crime."
You'll call this "racial profiling."
"Thin ice," they'll say.

You'll spend thirty years in the slammer, miss your daughter's
graduation and the Olympics. You'll start sleeping
under the railroad bridge, selling flowers to tourists,
saving up enough for bus fare, you'll sit by drunk women,
hide their handbags, tell everyone you
"saw her leaving it there *on purpose.*"

THE HISTORY OF BOOBY TRAPS

You were the worst suit I ever wore,
all gabardine itch with lynch collar.
The night your father became a Ghillie,
you set out for Minnesota with a fishing net,
forgetting your brass button on my nightgown
like an accidental kiss.

"I want it back," you told me the next day in a text message.
"I will be back," I misread you from the start, thinking
this could really work. Maybe I could make it work

this time. I wore your button on my tongue for two days
praying it would burn tiny holes through my teeth,
tattoo my gums green, bind us somehow, display my
fidelity no matter who I smiled at. Instead,
I could taste you in my sinuses: salty
masochism. Nothing more.

The hours spent waiting for an ambush, smoking
outside of auntie's parlor, expecting to outwit
you like I am Wile E. Coyote behind a boulder.
No, I am Tom Waits, the blackjack gambler.
No,

I don't like the way you fit me, the way I want to strut
into town with you draped over my body. I know if I wait

long enough, I will just stumble upon you anyway
like buried treasure, or genitals, or bait.

I never think to back down, let you go.
I never think to look down until everything
starts crashing on me, only then it's clear: I never
had the pull string in the first place. So like a chump
I go on standing on a great X with nothing to hold

but all my breaths.

BLACK.EARTH.LING.

>Found poetry from *The Jungle Book*
>by Rudyard Kipling (1894)

I.
he was trying to purchase
the full grown
gave a scolding and said
>*worthless*

he did not know much but was
the greatest whiteman in the world
a madman hunting wild
>*devils*

II.
and we will march on smooth roads
but son i am angry in the business
>that will rope
>a mere man
>his family
>to be trodden
>in the dirt of a
>bad one wicked
>one worthless son
>bah shame go they
>have said and perhaps
>and perhaps and perhaps who
>>knows
>as each man   joined the line

                stood ready   the catchers and
                hunters and   beaters the men
                who stayed   in the back
with their guns across their
arms and laughed
to a friend of his and broke
into a roar of laughter

                                      boys hang-
                                      ing eight
                                      feet up
                                      in the air

III.
remember though
that there are great
flat places hidden
away that are called
elephant ballrooms
but even these are found
only by accident

and no man
has ever seen
the silver four
piece mother
nursing baby

they were
rolled down
the plains

too happy
to speak
of such moon-
shine about
dances and
elephants

GROUND

n., adj., v. /graʊnd/
1. The ending. *Ashes to ashes, dust to dust*, etc.
2. Where the hungry spread their cardboard before wrapping their bones each night.
3. Earth's smile, her eye wrinkles, her warts and scars. Skin.
4. An excuse for wars, a place for wars. What people kill to cover.
5. Where pieces of today go to die. Where their survivors go to remember. See *"Ground Zero," tombs*, and *memorial halls*.
6. The result of grinding. Pulverising. The results of pillaging.
7. The beginning of all things. The evolution of mankind. Poetry. God. *From the ground up*. See also, *moon rocks, dirt* and *sacrifice*.

SLIPPERS ON THE SHELF

I, too, have seen the gold
      of November sunsets
      and I have conquered the holy
      grail of satisfaction.
I have deciphered the writhing skies,
      and the masochistic prairies,
      and I have seen, I've seen it all.

I have traveled by foot to neighboring towns and danced
      with the homeless around the fire.
I have fed Styx, the river, my coat
      when the water said to float, because
      it was not time. It was not time.
So, now I have seen, I've seen it all.

I have heard the reverberation
      of a revolver's bullet
      cracking echoes
      and lodging into brain juices
      of black strangers,
      (splattering purple sludge
      over pavement) and in time
I have seen someone's baby break.
I have felt this enormous world quake
      and I never knew why.
So, I have tangled my hair
      with clusters of thoughts

       because I have seen, I've seen it all.

I have trudged cautiously,
       aware of glass beneath puddles.
I have choked my mind
       in needless static
       and counted every prick.
I have judged a judge,
       and damned a god,
       and laughed like I would fall apart.
       because I have seen, I've seen it all.

I have been spanked and sent to bed.
I have met my uncle, now dead.
I have forged in silence
       and never knew why.
I have scraped the mold
       with fragile teeth,
       and pillaged the past,
       and stomped my feet.
I have prattled,
       and babbled, and blundered (Oh! Bah!)
       because I have seen, I've seen it all.

I have seen Mother Moon blink,
       with her electric eyelash, a lonely wink.
And from this was spellbound, from this was choked.
I felt bones squeeze around my throat.
I have wheezed,
I have coughed with breathing cut short.

I have seen the dizzy circles of time tort and retort.
And being released from grasp,
    gasping for more
    and more, and more, and more, and more…
    (Oh! How I whine! Begging Chronos,
    please be constant with *my* time),
    but once I caught my breath or once my breath (   )
    caught me, with nowhere to run, I sat stunned.
Am I born for death,
    strung to the shadowy leash of that happy nightingale?
    Waking up slowly to moan and milk my sorrows
    because I have seen, I've seen it all?

I, too, have bathed
    and admired myself,
    finding my parts neatly tucked inside.
I have dribbled on sticks (and felt so silly).
I have dreamt some dreams and
I've fallen from trees
    because I never knew to fly
    (No, never could I fly).
I haven't a good knight, nor a fair maiden
    but I have been victorious, all the same,
    and I have seen, I've seen it all.

I have replaced my intellect
    for heartless passion
    and brushed my teeth after every such occasion.
I have made a lion purr.

I have listened when my body said to
        stop.
I have listened when my body rolled itself
        on top of its lover to whisper,
        "It is not time, it is not time.
        Taste this moment. Breathe in the wine,"
        before easing back down to sleep.
So, I have seen, I've seen it all.

I have cried for you
        and never knew why.
I have cried for me
        (I've cried for me more).
I have wallowed in shame,
        then killed my own name,
        but grew myself another one.
And I have seen, I've seen it all.

With a pair of children's
        safety scissors, blue and small,
         I have cut the feet off Great Granddaddy
        Longlegs and studied his convulsive star.
And I have seen the moon bleeding
        puddles and I never asked her, "Why?"
For fifteen years I have nursed the wounds
        of womanhood and never earned
        my medal.
For thirty-eight years I will bleed puddles
        on my own (like the moon, on her own)
        and I have seen, I've seen it all.

I have saved your life
      and never knew why.
I have lost
      my mind.
I have lost
      my voice.
ihavelostmy (   ) breath.
I've lost but never died, I never died
      and I never knew why…

And now I loaf, observing, waiting.
Each year fading into fragments
      of frivols, and failures, and knowledge.
And I refuse to read all this drivel I write.

Oh pity! Tea time is over!
But I cannot adjourn until I break
      this bread.
I'm waiting,
      investing in every puff of a pause.
Waiting.
      remindingmyselfnotoforgetto- (   ) inhale.
Folding up my shawl
      and boxing up my slippers
      and all the while still uncertain
      where I went wrong
      and if I'm alright.
Waiting—
      before I snap off these lights
      and mutter an empty "g'night".

Waiting,
    waiting still,
    for the constant ticking
    of today to stop
    then burst
    because I have seen, I've seen it all.

Am I some crone? Am I alone
    on this minecart's descent? Waxing
    the coal of Aidoneus into selenite? Hacking
    on wafts of soot and cradling my haggard dreams
    though this darkened tunnel?

It matters not.

Despite all I have seen,
    in daylight I grow cold
    and I grow
    cold.

Damn! I haven't seen
    Lord Chronos retire,
    but I still don't believe
    my time will expire.

I have seen more war.
And I have seen a door.
And I can see (   )

a beam.

ACKNOWLEDGEMENTS:

My dear reader, you deserve my deepest gratitude. You have picked up this book, read the title and brought it in closer. Just look at you! You are extraordinary. You will take some risks, some irreversible twists. Just take a good look at yourself. Breathtaking, the way you hold onto this book, like you are carrying something as astonishing as yourself. For you, I give a wink.

I want to extend a gracious nod to Samantha Futhey for her editorial guidance, and also to Steve Semken (Ice Cube Press founder) and Debra Marquart (contest judge) for selecting this manuscript for the Prairie Seed Poetry Prize. Together, you all have helped paint these walls, hung the pictures and pointed when I broke too much glass—exactly what I've needed. Cheers!

Smooches to my main muses: Marsha Mae (cover artist) the original Jonesy, Ray Chay, Jordano, Ariana, Caitlin, Derek, Jazz's entire family, Jasmine, my mama and all the other sunflowers back in Kansas, who sometimes strut across these pages.

A curtsy goes to Benjamin and Sidney of *Storm Cellar* for grabbing, pulling, and allowing everything to ricochet into place. Without you, I'd still be chasing a Pushcart instead of dancing in its filthy buggy with a prize.

SEA SHARP is a Pushcart Prize winner (2017), a Hammer and Tongue poetry slam finalist (Brighton, 2015/16), and Prairie Seed Poetry Prize winner (2015/16). They are a Kansas State University graduate with a Bachelor of Arts degree in Creative Writing and Literature and minor degrees in Theatre and also Women's Studies. Sharp was the first poet featured on the Black Vegans Rock website (launched in 2016). They are passionate about intersectional veganism, black feminism, and other social movements that actively work towards empowering marginalised people, whilst dismantling all forms of oppression.

Sharp is Afro-Native American, LGBTQ+, a self-proclaimed "refugee of Kansas," and also a naturalised British citizen who lives in East Sussex with their husband.

Please visit Sea Sharp's website: www.seathepoet.com or follow them on most social media: @SeaThePoet

The Ice Cube Press **Prairie Seed Poetry Prize** celebrates the use of poetry to explore and better understand the history, people, culture, folklore, and themes of living in the United States Heartland.

The Ice Cube Press began publishing in 1993 to focus on how to live with the natural world and to better understand how people can best live together in the communities they share and inhabit. Using the literary arts to explore life and experiences in the heartland of the United States we have been recognized by a number of well-known writers including: Gary Snyder, Gene Logsdon, Wes Jackson, Patricia Hampl, Greg Brown, Jim Harrison, Annie Dillard, Ken Burns, Roz Chast, Jane Hamilton, Daniel Menaker, Kathleen Norris, Janisse Ray, Craig Lesley, Alison Deming, Harriet Lerner, Richard Rhodes, Michael Pollan, David Abram, David Orr, and Barry Lopez. We've published a number of well-known authors including: Mary Swander, Jim Heynen, Mary Pipher, Bill Holm, Connie Mutel, John T. Price, Carol Bly, Marvin Bell, Debra Marquart, Ted Kooser, Stephanie Mills, Bill McKibben, Pam Houston, Craig Lesley, Elizabeth McCracken, Dean Bakopoulos, and Paul Gruchow. Check out Ice Cube Press books on our web site, join our facebook group, follow us on twitter, visit booksellers, museum shops, or any place you can find good books and discover why we continue striving to, "hear the other side."

Ice Cube Press, LLC (est. 1993)
205 N. Front Street
North Liberty, Iowa 52317-9302
steve@icecubepress.com
twitter @icecubepress
www.icecubepress.com

to Laura Lee & Fenna Marie
dancing struting swaying
and
a w a y